FARBTESTSEITE

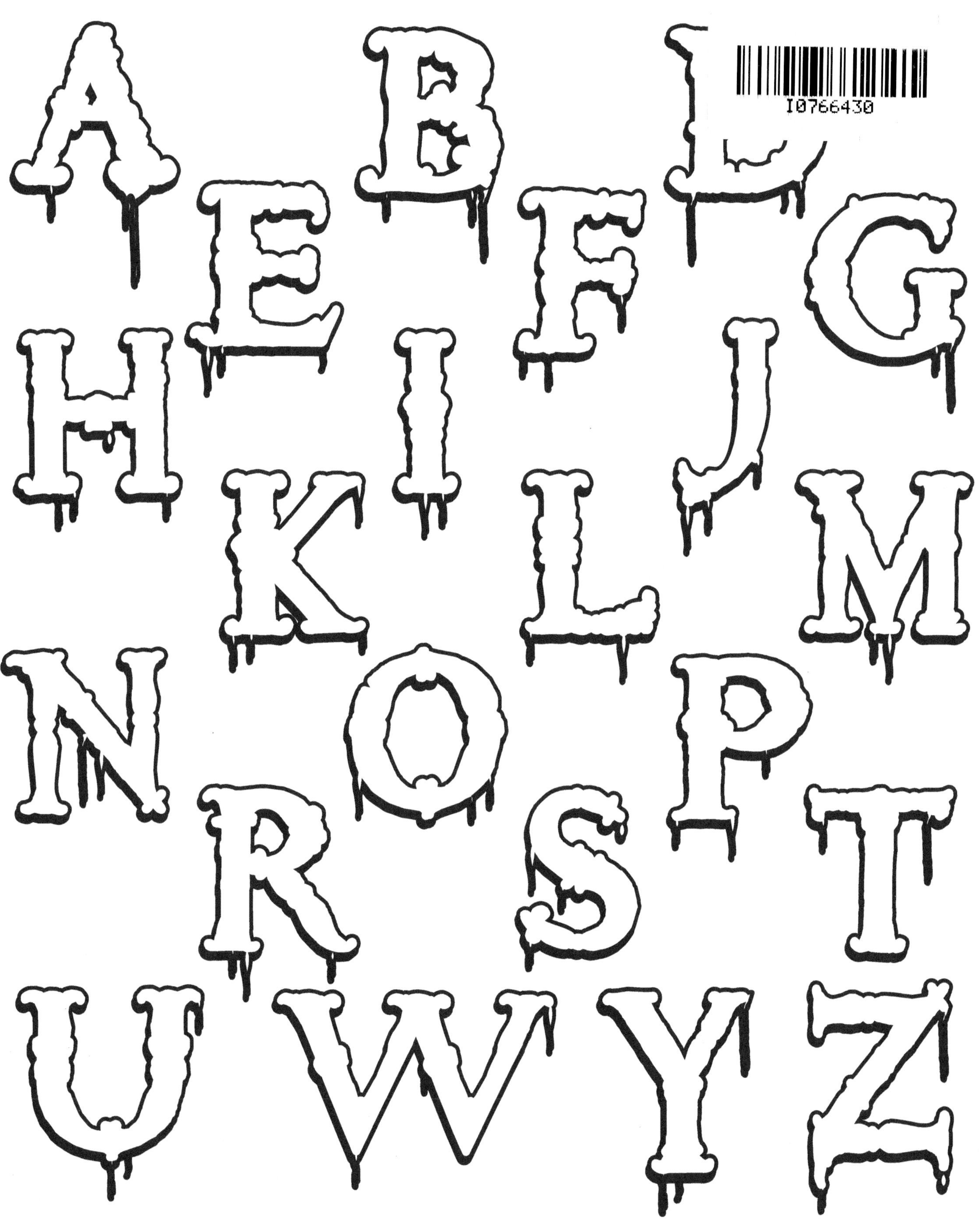

ALBRIGHT, CHARLES
3

BUNDY, TED 100

DAHMER, JEFFREY
17

ESCOBAR, PABLO
244

FISH, ALBERT
100+

GEIN, ED
2

HEIDNIK, GARY M.
2

IQBAL, JAVED
100

JONES, GENENE
60

Kürten, Peter
'69

LONG BOBBY JOE
10

MANSON, CHARLES
10+

MANSON, CHARLES
10+

NICHOLS, TERRY
176+

УКРАЇНА
NOPRIJENKO, ANATOLIJ
10
52

Pickton, Robert
49

RAMIREZ, RICARDO
19

SHAWCROSS, ARTHUR

TCHIKATILO ANDREI
'53

TOOLE OTTIS
125

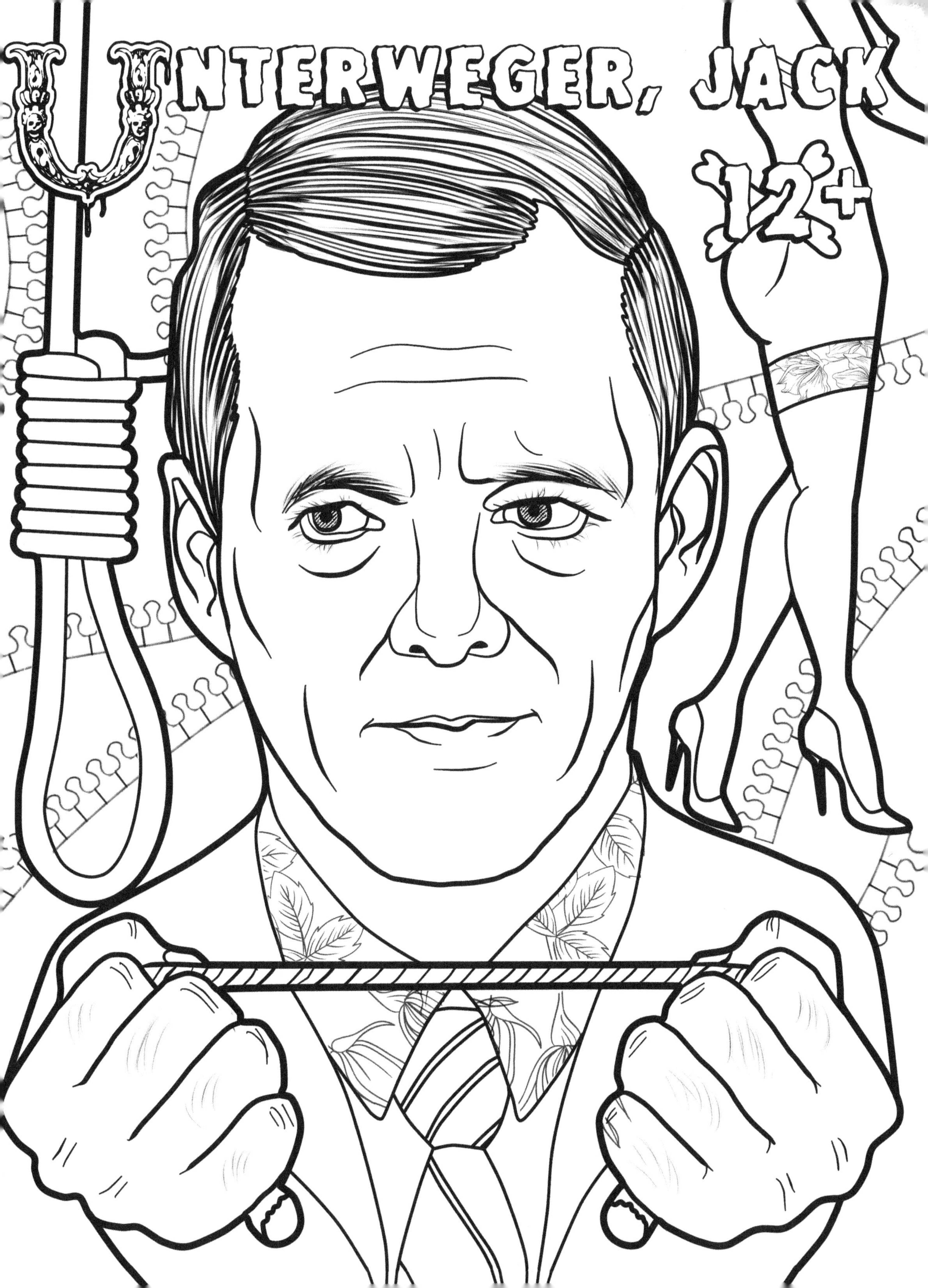

Unterweger, Jack
12+

WUORNOS, AILEEN
THE NATIONAL BANK
100
NH 123456789O
ONE WUMCARD

YOUNG, GRAHAM
3+

ZODIAC KILLER
5+
NEWS

AMERICAN FEMALE
SERIAL KILLERS
9
1982
1988
Potion pills
OVER
60
KILLERS
TO COLOR
Coloring Book for Adults
https://www.amazon.com/dp/9526925548

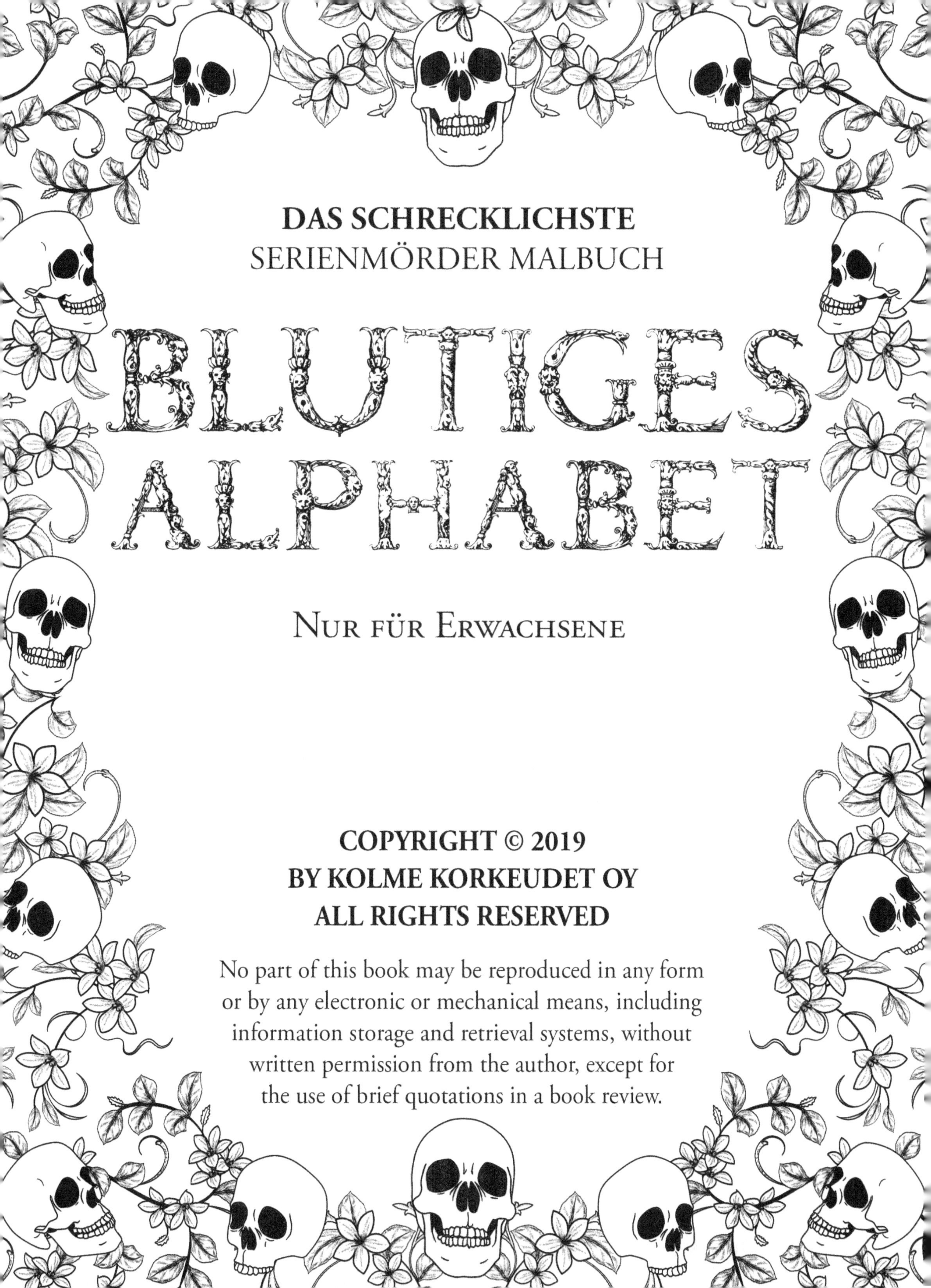

DAS SCHRECKLICHSTE
SERIENMÖRDER MALBUCH

BLUTIGES ALPHABET

Nur für Erwachsene

COPYRIGHT © 2019
BY KOLME KORKEUDET OY
ALL RIGHTS RESERVED

No part of this book may be reproduced in any form
or by any electronic or mechanical means, including
information storage and retrieval systems, without
written permission from the author, except for
the use of brief quotations in a book review.